# Bright Lights
# BIG CITY

Bright Lights Big City
A 21-Day Devotional About Shining the Light of Jesus
Published by Orange, a division of The reThink Group, Inc.
5870 Charlotte Lane, Suite 300
Cumming, GA 30040

The Orange logo is a registered trademark of The reThink Group, Inc
All rights reserved. Except for brief excerpts for review purposes, no part of this book may be reproduced or used in any form without written permission from the publisher.

Scripture quotations marked (NIV) are taken from the Holy Bible, New International Version®, NIV®. Copyright © 1973, 1978, 1984, 2011 by Biblica, Inc.™ Used by permission of Zondervan. All rights reserved worldwide. www.zondervan.com The "NIV" and "New International Version" are trademarks registered in the United States Patent and Trademark Office by Biblica, Inc.™

Scripture quotations are taken from the Holy Bible, New Living Translation (NLT), Copyright © 1996, 2004, 2015 by Tyndale House Foundation. Used by permission of Tyndale House Publishers, Inc., Carol Stream, Illinois 60188. All rights reserved.

Other Orange Products are available online and direct from the publisher at thinkorange.com.
Bulk copies are available at store.thinkorange.com

ISBN: 978-1-63570-232-3
© 2024 The reThink Group, Inc

Contributors: Leslie Mack, Dan Scott, Danielle Wilkins

Printed in the United States of America
First Edition 2024
1 2 3 4 5 6 7 8 9 10
07/15/24

**A 21-DAY DEVOTIONAL ABOUT SHINING THE LIGHT OF JESUS**

**IN MATTHEW 5:14, JESUS DESCRIBES US ALL WHEN HE SAYS: "YOU ARE THE LIGHT OF THE WORLD—LIKE A CITY ON A HILLTOP THAT CANNOT BE HIDDEN."**

**In this three-week devotional, our hope is that you would start to understand what it means for you to be the light of the world.**

*Like bright lights in a big city for all to see.*

God created you to shine—in your classrooms, in your home, in the theater cast, marching band, or on your team—by the way you bring light and hope into a world that seems chaotic at times.

In week one, we'll take a deep dive into how God created you to shine. The question isn't whether or not you will shine in the darkness of the world—that's a given. God created you to shine. Instead, the question is *how* will you shine like stars?

How will you shine when you interact with friends and family? How will you radiate God's light and love in the things you post on social media?

Next, when God declared, "Let there be light" in the creation story, God didn't simply shine a light into the darkness—God brought order to chaos. And God designed you to do the same. In week two, we'll explore how God uses all of us to bring order, peace, and light into the world around us.

And finally, in week three, we hope you discover more about what it means to see the world like God sees it. Jesus teaches us that when your perspective is generous, you'll find a whole new way of understanding the world. You'll start looking out to see the needs of people around you. You'll focus on ways to be generous and supportive, see people who need encouragement, and spot those who need compassion and grace. As you move to support and comfort them, your good deeds will shine for all to see.

As you read *Bright Lights, Big City,* think about this: How does following the way of Jesus affect the world around me?

We're praying for a great few weeks for you as you dive into *Bright Lights, Big City*. We can't wait to see how thinking about this changes you, your community, and even the world!

# GOD MADE YOU TO SHINE

## *Week 1*

Matthew 5:14-16 NLT, Philippians 2:15 NLT, 1 John 1:5 NLT

# HAVE YOU EVER BEEN TO A BIG CITY?

Maybe you live in a big city. Maybe you're growing up right outside of a big city and you always love when you get the chance to visit. Maybe you enjoy the chance to drive through and see the stadium lights after a big win or look up in the sky to see the beautiful city lights.

Now, this may feel like a strange turn, but stay with me. What if you discovered that God created us to live like big city lights? What if the energy you feel from places like New York City or Chicago is the same life-giving energy that people in your home, school, friend group, and team need from you?

And what if I told you that God has perfectly equipped you to display that energy for all to see?

It's true. God made you to shine!

And right now, our world needs light and life in a big way!

## Week 1

# DAY 1

**Bright Lights, Big City**

"Then God said, "Let there be light," and there was light. And God saw that the light was good. Then he separated the light from the darkness."

GENESIS 1:3-4 NLT

Have you ever used a night light? Sometimes, we use them out of fear of things we can't see. Other times, we just don't want to feel completely swallowed up by the dark. In the very beginning—before God created anything else—God made light, separating the day from the night. In God, there is no darkness at all. Because of that, we can trust that when we turn to God, there's nothing that won't be brought into the light. Every part of our hearts can be illuminated when we turn them over to the light of God.

**Have you ever been in total darkness? Think about the emotions you felt when faced with the total loss of light. What did you feel when you saw the light again? Take a moment and write about that below.**

**Each time you turn on a light this week, let it be a reminder to you that God is always with you, bringing light to every part of your life!**

**STEP 1: CAN YOU IDENTIFY AREAS IN YOUR LIFE THAT FEEL DARK? IF SO, WRITE THEM IN THE DARK SPACE.**

**STEP 2: USING THE LIGHT SPACE ABOVE, ASK GOD TO ILLUMINATE ANY AREAS IN YOUR LIFE THAT FEEL DARK!**

## Week 1

# DAY 2

**Bright Lights, Big City**

"Look up into the heavens. Who created all the stars? He brings them out like an army, one after another, calling each by its name. Because of his great power and incomparable strength, not a single one is missing."

ISAIAH 40:26 NLT

Did you know that God can give attention to everything created and not miss a single detail of it? Astronomers estimate that the universe could contain up to one septillion stars. (That's a one followed by 24 zeros!) Our Milky Way alone contains more than 100 billion. That means every star in the sky is known to God by name! In that limitless power, God knows the ins and outs of everything created, and that includes you! In the same way, God knows all of the stars, and God knows every detail of who you are.

**How does it feel knowing that God sees you, knows you, and loves you more than the incredible stars in the sky? Write down a few of your feelings in these stars.**

confident

## Week 1
# DAY 3

**Bright Lights, Big City**

"But you are not like that, for you are a chosen people. You are royal priests, a holy nation, God's very own possession. As a result, you can show others the goodness of God, for he called you out of the darkness into his wonderful light."

1 PETER 2:9 NLT

Not only does God know you by name, but God also calls you something amazing: *Child*. Not only are we called children of God, but we belong to God—and that means we can receive God's goodness and light. This is made possible through the death and resurrection of Jesus! His sacrifice on the cross made it possible for us to stand in the light of God. What's even cooler is that God doesn't just offer this gift to us; God wants us to show the people around us that they can receive this gift of light, too! This means our families, friends, next-door neighbors, and people we pass by at the grocery store!

## GOD CHOSE YOU!

Journal below about how it feels to know that God chose you.

God wants us to show the people around us that they can receive this gift too! Below each category, list a few quick ways you can share God's love with others this week . . .

| FAMILY | FRIENDS | NEIGHBOR | GROCERY STORE |
|---|---|---|---|
| | | | |

*Week 1*

# DAY 4

**Bright Lights, Big City**

"And we know that God causes everything to work together for the good of those who love God and are called according to his purpose for them."

ROMANS 8:28 NLT

Did you know God has created you on purpose, *for* a purpose? When you choose to follow Jesus with your life, you're choosing to bring light into the dark places in this world. While this is true for anyone and everyone who follows Jesus with their lives, it's still personal for you. God has created you for a specific purpose that only you can fulfill—a way to share the light of the Lord that is unique to you. When you step out in faith and share God's light with others—even when it's intimidating or you're unsure how it will go—you can trust that God will use your words, your heart, and your life for good.

What stops you from sharing your gifts and talents with others? Circle any that apply to you, and add more if you'd like!

- **Worried about what others might think**
- **Feel like I'm not good enough**
- **Afraid of being judged**
- **Worried I'll be embarrassed**

- _____
- _____
- _____
- _____

Let's be real—sometimes it can feel uncomfortable to share our gifts and talents. But trusting God can look like bringing YOUR light into dark places in a way only you can, even when it's intimidating! It's special because God gave you your gifts and talents so uniquely, and God can help you share them with others.

Write out a prayer. Ask God to help you see the specific gifts and talents you have to share the light of Jesus. Then, ask God for the courage to share them with others this week!

# Week 1
# DAY 5

**Bright Lights, Big City**

"For you were once darkness, but now you are light in the Lord. Live as children of light."

EPHESIANS 5:8 NIV

In Scripture, we find out that Jesus often talked about the importance of shining our light and living a life that's worthy of praise for the Lord. Later, Paul echoed this idea in his letter to the people of Ephesus. He said that while we are born into a world full of sin and darkness, in Christ, we can be free from the grip of this darkness. How? By putting our faith in Jesus, living for Him, and letting His light shine through us in how we act, talk, and live our lives. So, how do we live as children of the light? If we want to walk in the light, we must be devoted to developing an intimate relationship with Jesus by seeking Him every day.

When you think about seeking Jesus every day, what actions come to mind? *(Hint: you're doing one right now!)*

_____

_____

_____

**Talk to a trusted adult this week about how you can seek Jesus in everything you do. What can you do to step into His light and let it shine out of your life?**

# DAY 6

**Bright Lights, Big City**

*"Don't be afraid, for I am with you. Don't be discouraged, for I am your God. I will strengthen you and help you. I will hold you up with my victorious right hand."*

ISAIAH 41:10 NLT

The quickest thing that can dim our light? Fear! Whether it's fear of circumstances around us, fear of what may happen in the future, or just fear of being the person God made us to be, that fear can feel powerful when we face it. The good news? We can remember God's promises in Scripture to remind us we're not doing it alone. When we find ourselves feeling afraid, we can remember that God is always with us. That presence is our ultimate source of strength, power, and light in every moment—but especially in the moments when we're afraid. Even if you feel like you're up against impossible circumstances, help is no further than your next breath because God is always near.

Write this verse on a sticky note and stick it somewhere you'll see it often—like on your lamp, a mirror, or on a binder. Let it remind you that God's light is always shining, even over your fears.

> "DON'T BE AFRAID, FOR I AM WITH YOU. DON'T BE DISCOURAGED, FOR I AM YOUR GOD. I WILL STRENGTHEN YOU AND HELP YOU. I WILL HOLD YOU UP WITH MY VICTORIOUS RIGHT HAND."
> ISAIAH 41:10, NLT

## Week 1
# DAY 7

**Bright Lights, Big City**

"In the same way, let your good deeds shine out for all to see, so that everyone will praise your heavenly Father."

MATTHEW 5:16 NLT

You know what's cool? You—yes, you—are part of God's plan to bring light into a dark, broken, and hurting world. Through your unique gifts and experiences, Jesus' light shines in you. The God Who created the universe in all its wonder is the same God who thinks you are even more brilliant. So, it's time to shine! Shine a light in your school, with your family, in your friendships, in Small Groups, and everywhere you go. Because you, my friend, were made to shine!

**This week, take a moment to make a list of three things you can do to uniquely shine God's light into your community, then share it with someone who can encourage you while you shine!**

# I CAN SHINE GOD'S LIGHT IN MY COMMUNITY BY . . .

★

★ _____

★ _____

# GOD'S LIGHT IN YOU BRINGS ORDER TO CHAOS

*Week 2*

# HAVE YOU EVER LOOKED AROUND AT WHAT'S HAPPENING IN THE WORLD?

I mean, there's A LOT going on right now! The impact of climate change. The way people are treated for being different. The constant threat of war starting somewhere in the world. Not to mention the adults who can't agree on how to solve it all.

All of it can feel discouraging, overwhelming . . . chaotic.

You might wonder how you can help or if it even matters if you *try* to help.

You're not alone. Lots of people feel this way. Thankfully, when you start to read the Bible, you can find wisdom that can help you discover how you can help when things feel so broken.

Did you know that at the very beginning of the creation story, God didn't just speak to create light in the darkness? God did so much more than that . . . in that moment, God brought order to chaos.

But this wasn't just a one-time moment back at the creation of the universe. This is something God has continued doing ever since.

God is in the business of bringing order to chaos.

On top of that, God invites you, me—everyone really—to play a part in this work.

That's right! God can use YOU to bring order to chaos, peace to conflict, and light to a world that feels so dark sometimes.

This week, we'll discover how that can look as you try to follow Jesus every day. So . . . what are you waiting for? Turn the page and find out!

*Week 2*

# DAY 1

**Bright Lights, Big City**

"Now the earth was formless and empty, darkness was over the surface of the deep, and the Spirit of God was hovering over the waters. And God said, 'Let there be light,' and there was light. God saw that the light was good, and he separated the light from the darkness."

GENESIS 1:2-4 NIV

Before God created the world, there was nothing. *God started with nothing, just total chaos and darkness over the world. How did it go from chaos to all the beauty we see around us?* God! God spoke light into the darkness and created order. What was once dark suddenly became full of light. Sometimes, we can forget the enormous power and strength of our God—the God who made something from nothing! God spoke the light into existence! God designed the universe and all its structure so that every piece of it would work together. And that includes us! The same light that God spoke into the world is the same light at work in us. It's the light that will bring calm to the chaos in our hearts if we let it.

**What is something in your life that feels like chaos? If you can think of something, write it down around the outside of the ball of chaos on the next page. Then, take a moment and ask God to help you bring calm to the chaos in your life. Then, in the orderly circle write, "God's light brings calm to my chaos."**

**Next time you're feeling like your world is spinning out of control, remember, God is with you and can help bring peace and calm to your situation.**

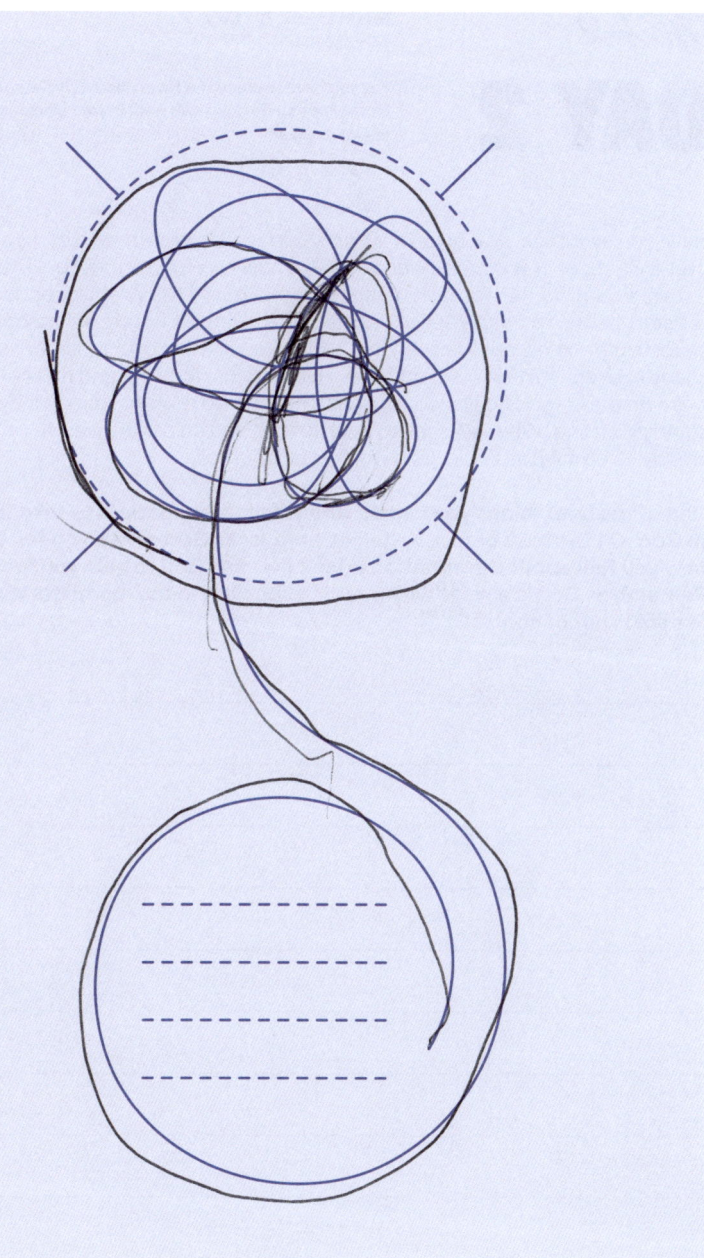

# DAY 2

**Bright Lights, Big City**

*"For you have rescued me from death; you have kept my feet from slipping. So now I can walk in your presence, O God, in your life-giving light."*

PSALM 56:13 NLT

Have you ever tried walking on a slippery surface? Maybe it was across an ice patch or over a wet floor. If you have, then you know how careful you must be! Every time you try to take a step, you're worried your feet will move in all the wrong directions, your arms will start flailing to try to keep your balance, and it feels like you're about to fall. It's total chaos! Sometimes, our lives can feel a lot like navigating over a slippery surface. With chaos at every turn—in our relationships, emotions, families, and more—it feels like we're on the verge of collapse. The good news is we don't have to wonder how to stay standing strong. When we look to God for light and guidance, we can be sure we'll stay steady. Even if we stumble, God won't ever let us fall.

**One of the best things you can do when life feels chaotic is to take time and pray to God. On the lines below, write out a prayer to God where you tell God all about how you feel about the situation in your life. Ask God to help you feel at peace. Remember, God is always with you . . . especially in the moments when you feel like life is out of control.**

*Week 2*

# DAY 3

**Bright Lights, Big City**

"Jesus spoke to the people once more and said, "I am the light of the world. If you follow me, you won't have to walk in darkness, because you will have the light that leads to life."

JOHN 8:12 NLT

Sometimes, the world can seem like a scary place. On the news, on social media, in our own lives, in the lives of others—all around us, we see things that feel like darkness. In other words, we see sad, hard, hurtful things happening all the time. And while that can be incredibly overwhelming, as followers of Jesus, we have the reminder that the darkness in this world doesn't win. Jesus tells us that when we follow Him, we can walk in the light. Not just any light, but His light—the light of the world that will lead us to the full life God has for us.

**In the box below, write out John 8:12. Use your most expressive handwriting or decorate it with doodles and drawings. Underline the word "light" so it stands out to you. When you've finished all the readings for this week, cut out your drawing and hang it up where you can see it every morning before you head out for the day. Be reminded that Jesus can help you stay in the light and experience the best life God has for you!**

# DAY 4

**Bright Lights, Big City**

"Feed the hungry, and help those in trouble. Then your light will shine out from the darkness, and the darkness around you will be as bright as noon."

ISAIAH 58:10 NLT

Scripture promises that when we follow Jesus, we can walk in the light. We don't have to wander lost or unsure of what direction to go. What's more, we also know that when we trust God, we can be filled with that same light. The very same light that Jesus brought to the world can be alive in us. When we do things to serve and love others—when we help the people around us in trouble—we're doing more than just supporting and caring for them. We're shining the light of Jesus into the darkness of their situation and in the way we live and love. Pretty cool, right?

**This week, think about the people in your life. Consider how you can brighten their day. Look at the descriptions below. Write down a person who comes to mind who might be experiencing something similar.**

- **Feeling sad** _____
- **Excited about something** _____
- **Having a difficult time** _____
- **Needs a friend** _____
- **Struggling in school** _____
- **Got a new pet** _____
- **Is busy with chores** _____

**How can you serve a few of those people this week? Make a plan to connect with at least one of them, shine God's light, and show them how much you care about them!**

*Week 2*

# DAY 5

**Bright Lights, Big City**

"The light shines in the darkness, and the darkness can never extinguish it."

JOHN 1:5 NLT

In Scripture, a contrast between the light and the darkness is clearly displayed throughout its pages. But what does this mean? Light represents God's goodness shining through Jesus, while darkness represents the sins of the world. A life of darkness is depressing, sorrowful, lonely, and hurtful. But thankfully, we aren't stuck in that life. When we allow Jesus to come into our lives, we can be free from the grip of darkness and sin that has a hold on us. We can have hope because of Jesus. He came to bring the light of God into a spiritually dark and dying world. He gives us the freedom from our harmful desires, struggles, hurts, and sins. So, if we follow Jesus, we don't have to live in darkness any longer!

**Head to a room where you live that can get really, really dark. Turn off all the lights, then . . . try to read John 1:5 from the top of this page.**

**Not too easy, right? Maybe if you have some light creeping in from a window or the hallway outside, you could see the page a little bit. But more than likely, the verse was hard to read.**

**Now, turn on one light in the room. How much can you see around you with just that candle lighting up the dark room? Can you see enough to read? If so, read John 1:5 again.**

**This is how people see you every time you share God's love with them. Using kind words, sharing about what God is doing in your life, and even simply being there while a friend is hurting—all of those things can offer the sort of hope people need to see that God's light is still shining in the dark.**

**Find a way to be a light to someone today.**

**Bright Lights, Big City**

> "Feed the hungry, and help those in trouble. Then your light will shine out from the darkness, and the darkness around you will be as bright as noon."
>
> ISAIAH 58:10 NLT

Have you ever turned on a light in a dark room? Before you did, it was probably hard to see. In the darkness, you didn't know where to go. You might've even felt a little scared! Then suddenly, there was light. Just like that, it all became clear. You felt safe to move around again without fear of what you couldn't see before. When we allow God into our lives, God's light does the same for us. It shines in us and through us to light up our whole lives. Not only does it help us see where to go and what to do, but it can also light the way for others. When we let God's light shine in our lives, we're not just opening ourselves up to more confidence and joy; we're opening others up to it, too!

**Who in your life do you want to be a light to? Take a look back at your list of people from Day 4 this week. Choose one of those people and make a plan below for how you can be a light and show them God's love this week.**

1. _____
2. _____
3. _____
4. _____
5. _____
6. _____

**Pray that God will show you how you can share God's light with this person this week.**

## Week 2
# DAY 7

**Bright Lights, Big City**

"In the same way, let your good deeds shine out for all to see, so that everyone will praise your heavenly Father."

MATTHEW 5:16 NLT

Jesus tells us that serving others and doing good is how we shine our light. That's a pretty big deal, right? Well, Jesus didn't leave it there. He also reminds us that when we shine that light, it's not about us. The good things we do for others aren't for our own reward or glory. It isn't about making us look good. Rather, it's about reflecting the light and love of God to those around us. When we do good deeds, we do them to shine God's light into the world and point others back to God's love for them.

**Read Matthew 5:16, several times in a row. Then, in the box below, draw how you imagine a city on a hill shining a light in the world around it. Write out the words to Matthew 5:16 as a border around the box, see if you can write it from memory! Work on memorizing it this week to always remember that God invites you to shine the light of Jesus in the world around you!**

# GOD'S LIGHT IN YOU BRINGS LIGHT TO OTHERS

*Week 3*

# MAYBE THERE'S SOMETHING IN YOU THAT WANTS TO BE THE PERSON WHO SHINES A LIGHT TO HELP SOMEONE ELSE.

Have you ever thought about how many people we walk by every single day who, in one way or another, need someone to bring light into their lives.

I think if we pay enough attention, we can see that our world has quite a bit of darkness that could use God's light. When we learn about what's going on in the world on social media, hear our family talking, or start a new unit at school, it can feel like the areas that need God's light are endless! Disease, war, poverty, inequality, violence, starvation . . . the list goes on and on.

Maybe, you feel like you're in darkness in your own home. It feels like a combat zone at times. Maybe it's the fact that you have a younger or older sibling who creates chaos for the whole house. Or maybe your parents are struggling. Maybe you don't get along with your stepdad, stepmom, or caregiver.

Maybe you feel like there's darkness in your friend group. Maybe you're realizing the friends you hang with most are the people who get you in the most trouble. Or maybe the darkness you feel is that you wish you had a good, trustworthy friend. You feel all alone. No one knows the real you. Darkness for you is best described as loneliness.

It could be you feel like you're surrounded by darkness as it relates to how you see yourself. I think we'd all agree that we're living in a brutal storm of constant comparison. The more you compare yourself to images and ideas that society considers the standard, the more it feels like you slip into darkness. Grades. Body image. Friends. Likes on social media. Clothes. Shoes. The more you feel like you don't measure up, the darker it seems to get, right?

Or maybe you see the darkness enveloping a friend, a family member, or someone who means a lot to you. You so desperately want them to feel loved, supported, and cared for. You want them to see the light.

Maybe there's something in you that wants to be the person who shines a light to help someone else.

If that's you, there's a reason you feel that way.

## Week 3
# DAY 1

**Bright Lights, Big City**

"Your eye is like a lamp that provides light for your body. When your eye is healthy, your whole body is filled with light."

MATTHEW 6:22 NLT

Have you ever walked into a dark room, and the shadows made everything look creepy? Once you turned on the light, you probably gained a lot more confidence in the space you were in. That's because perspective can change everything. Everything looks different in the light. Jesus tells us that our eyes are the lamps of our bodies. It's a strange way to say that how we see the world is important. When we see it through our own lens, it may feel unclear, scary, or even overwhelming at times. But when we see it through the lens of God, everything becomes clear. Then, our whole perspective changes!

**Today, take time to ask God to help you see the world through the lens of God's light. Pray that you will have that perspective as you move through this week.**

# TRAIN YOURSELF TO SPOT HOW GOD IS WORKING EVERY DAY!

Practice looking for God at work in the world around you everyday. Read the following scenarios. In the blank space write one way you can see a character trait of God in that situation.

| SCENARIO | GOD TRAITS |
|---|---|
| You see someone save a seat at lunch for the newest kid at your school. | God wants everyone to be included and connected to others. |
| A person picks up litter and tosses it into a nearby trash can. | |
| Your parent sets up a family rule to not use certain websites to help you learn to be safe around strangers online. | |
| You make signs to put up around your neighborhood of a lost pet you found. | |

**How can seeing the world through the lens of Jesus change how you see the world?**

## Week 3
# DAY 2

**Bright Lights, Big City**

"This is my command—be strong and courageous! Do not be afraid or discouraged. For the Lord your God is with you wherever you go."

JOSHUA 1:9 NLT

Do you ever feel pulled in two different directions? Maybe you have a friend encouraging you to make a certain choice while a parent is encouraging you to make a different one. Maybe you want to choose one way for yourself, but everybody else in your life seems to be telling you to go the other way. Whatever it is, when we feel unsure of what to do or where to go, it can be confusing to know who to listen to. The good news is that God wants to be with us when we face challenging decisions. No matter what decision we're trying to make or what path we're trying to walk, we can trust that God can shed light in the right direction. When we focus on that, we can trust that we're going to make the best decision for our lives. Why? Because it's a decision led by God's light!

**If you're struggling with a decision or you're uncertain about what to do in a situation in your life right now, write it down in the box below.**

**Then, take it to God. Ask that God lead you with God's light in the best direction for your life. Use the "Tough Decision Help Kit" on the next page as a way to help you make your next big decision.**

# TOUGH DECISION HELP KIT

**NAMES OF 3 PEOPLE I CAN GO TO FOR WISE ADVICE**

1. 
2. 
3. 

**I AM BETTER AT MAKING WISE CHOICES**

IN THE DAY TIME

IN THE NIGHT TIME

**CIRCLE 3 THINGS I CAN DO TO HELP ME THINK CLEARLY AND WEIGH MY OPTIONS**

- DRAW A PICTURE
- TALK TO A FRIEND
- TALK TO AN ADULT
- WRITE IN A JOURNAL
- GO FOR A WALK
- WORKOUT TO CLEAR MY MIND
- LIST POSSIBLE REALISTIC OUTCOMES
- TALK TO GOD
- READ SCRIPTURE

**WRITE A PRAYER TO GOD. WE HELPED YOU GET STARTED:**

Dear God, It can be challenging to make decisions. It is comforting to know that you are always with me and will never leave me. Today I am thinking about . . .

## Week 3
# DAY 3

**Bright Lights, Big City**

"Don't be selfish; don't try to impress others. Be humble, thinking of others as better than yourselves. Don't look out only for your own interests, but take an interest in others, too."

PHILIPPIANS 2:3-4 NLT

Have you ever spoken up only to feel like no one was listening? Maybe it was in your Small Group, at the dinner table with your family, or in a hard conversation with a friend. If you've been there, then you know just how awful that feels. When you're trying to speak—but no one seems to be listening—it leaves you feeling dismissed, ignored, and unimportant. While you can't always change the fact that some may not take an interest in what you're saying, you can change the way you respond to and listen to others. When you're in the position to listen, support, and care for someone else, do it! Not just because you don't want to make them feel the way you've felt when it's happened to you, but because you know that this is part of what it means to follow Jesus, too! Jesus was a great example of treating others the way we'd want to be treated, and we get to practice doing that when we listen to others. That's part of shining the light of Jesus into the world, and it's something we can do simply in the way we support and show up for the people around us.

**Who in your life can you take time to listen to this week? Talk to an adult about how you can work on being a good listener. Support that person so you can shine God's light in their direction!**

# 4 LISTENING CUES

 **MAKE EYE CONTACT**

 **LEAN FORWARD**

 **ASK GREAT FOLLOW UP QUESTIONS**

 **PUT AWAY DISTRACTIONS**

## Week 3
## DAY 4

**Bright Lights, Big City**

*"So now I am giving you a new commandment: Love each other. Just as I have loved you, you should love each other."*

JOHN 13:34 NLT

Be honest with yourself: How easy is it for you to love other people? Your answer probably sounds something like, *"Well, it depends on who that other person is . . ."* That's true for all of us! The family members who love us, the friends who treat us well, the Small Group Leader who shows up for us, the coach who supports us—those people are easy to love. But the friend who betrayed us, the family member who's mean to us, the kid on the team who teases us, the teacher who is always harsh—those people don't make it easy. That's when Jesus' words come in handy for us. He reminds us that, as Christians, we can love anyone and everyone—those who make it easy and those who don't—because of Jesus' love in us. While we don't have to be close to everyone (especially those who have hurt us), we can show love to anyone simply in the way we think about, talk about, and treat them. That's how we can shine a little light!

**Today, think about a way you can practice loving the people around you and letting the light of Jesus shine through you as you do.**

**What are ways to show love to others?**
- Write a note
- Help with a chore
- Say something nice
- Create something for them
- _____
- _____

**What is one way to show love to others?**
- Even when you're mad. . .
- Even when you're disappointed. . .
- Even when you are busy. . .
- Even when you don't feel like talking. . .
- _____
- _____

**Journal prompt:** Who in your life who is not easy to love? What is one way you can show love to them?

*Week 3*

# DAY 5

**Bright Lights, Big City**

"In the same way, let your good deeds shine out for all to see, so that everyone will praise your heavenly Father."

MATTHEW 5:16 NLT

One of the biggest parts of our faith is to not just know the Bible but also had to live out God's Word every single day. Now, this might seem like a huge task, but God will give you the capabilities, gifts, and strength to fulfill God's purpose in your life. As Christians, we need to use the gifts God has given us to bring glory to God and be children of the light. We must live out our faith in our actions, words, and character so that others can see something unique in our hearts. Why cover our light and leave the world around us in the dark? Why would we have the greatest thing to offer the world only to cover it up, hide it, and not share it with others?

**Doodle some things that bring you joy.**

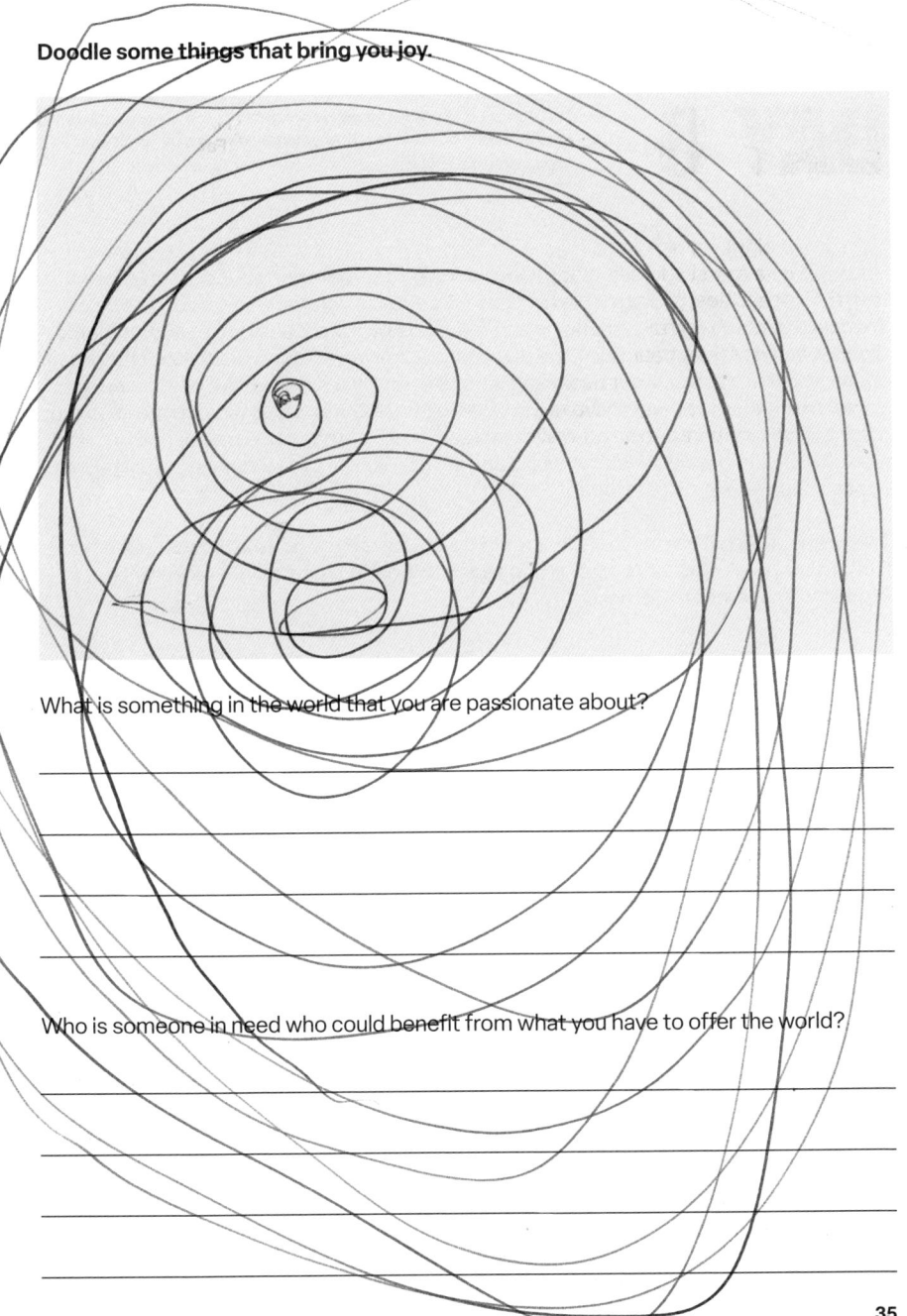

What is something in the world that you are passionate about?

_____
_____
_____
_____
_____

Who is someone in need who could benefit from what you have to offer the world?

_____
_____
_____
_____
_____

## Week 3
# DAY 6

**Bright Lights, Big City**

"But you are a chosen people, a royal priesthood, a holy nation, God's special possession, that you may declare the praises of him who called you out of darkness into his wonderful light."

1 PETER 2:9 NIV

Have you ever found yourself comparing yourself to someone in your class or on your team? Maybe even a sibling or close friend? It's easy to compare ourselves to others. We can look at the people around us and feel like they're so much better at something than we are, right? At the end of the day, that can leave us feeling pretty awful about ourselves. The reason? Well, because it's not the way we're meant to live! The truth is, we're all valued, unique, and loved in God's eyes. Nothing about who we are is meant to be compared to anyone else. Instead, we're all meant to use our unique gifts, personalities, and wiring with the world around us. We work together as God's children to shine God's light into the world.

**This week, talk with your friends about the unique gifts and talents you each have. Consider how you as a group can use those things to shine a little more of God's light into the world together.**

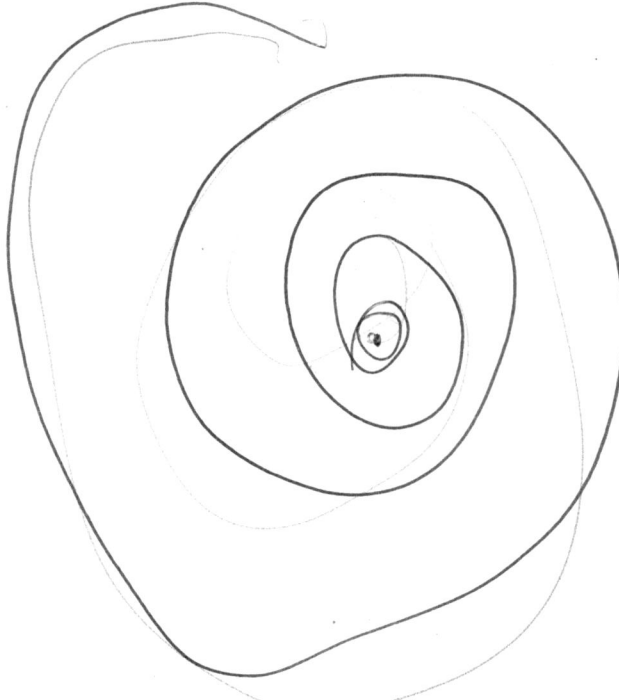

# WRITE DOWN THE WONDERFUL TRAITS OF YOU AND A FEW OF THE PEOPLE YOU KNOW

| MY NAME | FRIEND'S NAME | FRIEND'S NAME |
| --- | --- | --- |
| | | |

## Week 3

# DAY 7

**Bright Lights, Big City**

"In the same way, let your good deeds shine out for all to see, so that everyone will praise your heavenly Father."

MATTHEW 5:16 NLT

What are you passionate about? What do you love doing? It could be playing a sport, making music, reading books, writing stories, or creating masterpieces. Whatever it is, God has placed you in those spaces and communities for a reason. As children of God, we all have the chance to bring light into the spaces and places in our lives. Whether that's at home, at school, at practice, in public, or anywhere you might be, you can shine God's light to others by using your gifts for God's glory.

**Memorize Matthew 5:16.**

**Use symbol association to memorize it:**

Associate each part of the verse with a visual image in your mind. Draw those symbols somewhere you can see them.

Examples:
- "In the same way" – Doodle two objects that are the same.
- "Let your good deeds shine" – Draw a green check (good) and a lightbulb (shine).
- "Out for all to see" – Doodle a group of stick figures.
- "So that everyone will praise" – Doodle hands raised or an exclamation point.
- "Your father in heaven" – Doodle a mustache or a dad hat to remind you of father.

Now make up your own

Not a fan of drawing? Try one of these memorization techniques:
- Use a dry-erase marker to write it on a mirror you see often.
- Design a phone lock screen in your favorite app.
- Write a song, rap, or poem that helps you recite this verse on repeat.

# "IN THE SAME WAY, LET YOUR GOOD DEEDS SHINE OUT FOR ALL TO SEE, SO THAT EVERYONE WILL PRAISE YOUR HEAVENLY FATHER."
## MATTHEW 5:16 NLT

**EXAMPLE**

**YOUR TURN**

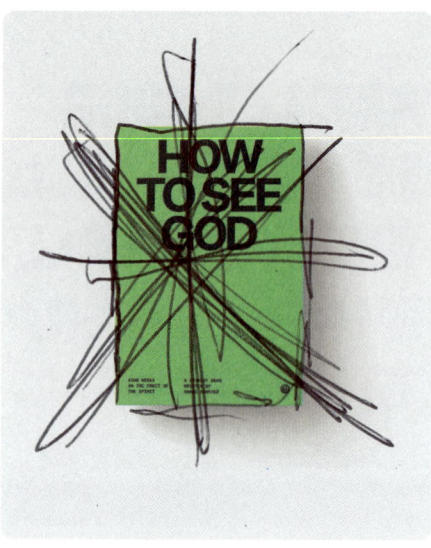

## How to See God: Four Weeks on the Fruit of the Spirit

*How To See God* is a four-week devotional guide for teenagers that helps them develop the skill of looking for God's Spirit at work in their everyday world. Through the fruit of the Spirit, they can begin to see what God is like and how God's Spirit shows up in themselves and in the people around them.

## Know God: A 28-Day Devotional Experience for Students

Know God is a devotional about starting students on a journey to help them know God more. Because even though there's no formula for knowing everything about God, there are a few things you can do every day that will help you know Him better.

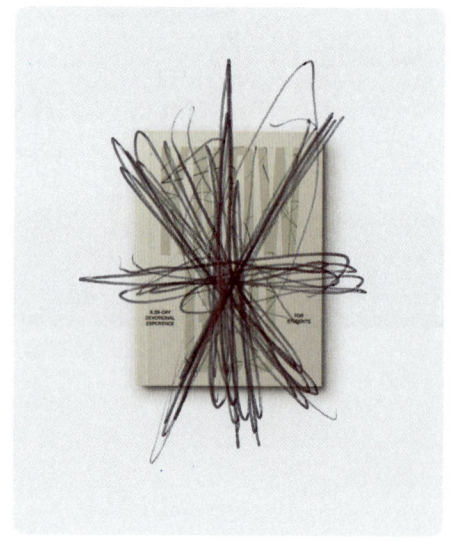

**Visit Store.ThinkOrange.com to learn more.**